alberto giacometti

# alberto giacometti

WITH AN INTRODUCTION *by Peter Selz* AND AN AUTOBIOGRAPHICAL
STATEMENT *by the artist* · THE MUSEUM OF MODERN ART, NEW YORK
*in collaboration with* THE ART INSTITUTE OF CHICAGO, THE LOS ANGELES
COUNTY MUSEUM OF ART, & THE SAN FRANCISCO MUSEUM OF ART

*distributed by Doubleday & Company, Garden City, New York*

For young painters and sculptors Alberto Giacometti occupies a position apart from that of all other living artists. His work, neither imitated nor slandered, is out of competition. Like a saint, he is placed in a niche by himself. "It is still possible to work like Giacometti," his younger colleagues say, taking comfort from his integrity as they proceed about their own business. Although his work, changing relatively little over a period of almost twenty years now, is very familiar, its resources are inexhaustible and the impact of his approach is inevasible.

On behalf of the Trustees of The Museum of Modern Art, the Art Institute of Chicago, the Los Angeles County Museum of Art, and the San Francisco Museum of Art, I wish to express my greatest gratitude to Alberto Giacometti himself for his gracious co-operation and the many hours he has given to me in Paris, in St.-Paul-de-Vence, and in Stampa. It is a pleasure to record my thanks to the museums and individuals (listed on page 120) who have graciously consented to part with their sculptures, paintings, or drawings for so long a period.

My sincere thanks are due Mr. Pierre Matisse for his untiring help and co-operation, to Miss Irene Gordon for supervising this publication, to Miss Alicia Legg for editing the catalogue, to Miss Therese Varveris for curatorial assistance, to Miss Inga Forslund for assembling the bibliography, and to Mr. Wilder Green for the installation of the exhibition in New York. I am also greatly indebted to the following persons, whose advice and co-operation greatly facilitated this undertaking: Mrs. Margaret Scolari Barr, Mr. Hans J. Bechtler, Miss Françoise Boas, M. Louis Clayeux, Mr. Kenneth Donahue, Miss Helen M. Franc, Mr. Abram Lerner, Mr. William S. Lieberman, M. Aimé Maeght, Mr. Herbert Matter, Mrs. Mercedes Matter, Mr. A. James Speyer, and Mr. David Sylvester.

Our gratitude is also extended for the special assistance rendered by the Alsdorf Foundation, the Joseph H. Hirshhorn Foundation, the Reader's Digest Association, Inc., and to Mr. William Inge and Mr. Joseph Pulitzer, Jr.

Peter Selz
*Director of the Exhibition*

"To render what the eye really sees is impossible," Giacometti repeated one evening while we were seated at dinner in the inn at Stampa. He explained that he could really not see me as I sat next to him —I was a conglomeration of vague and disconnected details—but that each member of the family sitting across the room was clearly visible, though diminutive, thin, surrounded by enormous slices of space. Everyone before him in the whole history of art, he continued, had always represented the figure as it is; his task now was to break down tradition and come to grips with the optical phenomenon of reality. What is the relationship of the figure to the enveloping space, of man to the void, even of being to nothingness?

The philosophical and emotional implications of the problem he poses do not overly concern him. The loneliness of his figures, that elusive quality upon which all his critics and admirers—it seems impossible to be one without being the other—have commented, is, in so far as he is concerned, the effect of *his* retinal vision. His friend Jean Genet, for example, has Giacometti's objects saying, "I am alone, I am transfixed in a necessity which you cannot disturb. As I am what I am, I am indestructible. Being what I am and without reservation, my solitude knows about your solitude." His figures may indeed evoke this feeling of loneliness and alienation, but this is by no means the artist's purpose. He strives to discover the visual appearance and to render it with precision—not the reflections of light which occupied the Impressionists, nor the distorted view of the camera which fails to register distance, but the object as it is contained in space, as seen by the human eye, the artist's eye.

The eye is man's miraculous instrument: it is both the mirror of self and its means of communication. Giacometti stares at people's eyes, hoping thus to understand them. He says that the blind seem to think with their eyes, and that the difference between a living person and a corpse is the gaze. In his painting and his sculpture he concentrates on the eye. "It should be enough to sculpt the eyes," he has said. In his painted portraits all the lines converge intensely on the eyes. If he could render a single eye correctly, he maintains, he would have the head, the figure, the world.

Jean-Paul Sartre has declared that "after three thousand years, the task of Giacometti and of contemporary sculptors is not to enrich the galleries with new work, but to prove that sculpture itself is still possible." Giacometti is aware of this predicament, and his attempts to resolve it have led him to the problem that absorbs him today—to render precisely what he sees at a given distance. This distance—which creates the space containing the object—has become absolute: it is about nine feet, the distance from which his glance, focusing on the model's eye, can organize the whole. The result is a pervasive presence. The figures—in his paintings, his drawings, his sculpture—become clearest when we focus on them least. A standing nude female figure or a head of Diego, becomes increasingly vague as we approach it. At close range, the nose, chin, breasts do not reveal themselves: they disintegrate and we are left only with a vital surface of light flickering over the rough bronze—crater-like surfaces which remain witnesses of the artist's struggle. But the figures retain their integrity. They do not allow us to come into intimate contact with them. They remain unreachable and can only be seen at the distance from which they were modeled or painted. Within the space that contains them, they become real. To be in a room with a figure by Giacometti is not to enjoy an object but to experience a presence.

Giacometti is constantly at work. His hands never rest but move up and down modeling the clay on the armature, drawing figures and hands on paper napkins, envelopes, table tops. His work is continuous. He draws, builds, destroys, paints, models—one activity leading into the other without interruption. Nothing is ever finished. When painting, he builds up, paints over, makes changes, and finally stops, hoping to achieve the goal next time. He may turn his clay models over to his brother Diego for casting, but when he sees the plaster he is likely to hack away at it and when confronted with the bronze, to paint on it, in a constant process of growth, or rather, search, that will never end. Like other artists of his generation he is engaged more in the adventure than concerned with the result. Each work is a step for him, a study for new work, for the task of achieving the impossible: to render reality truly as it appears to the eye and yet to make a sculpture or a painting which, somehow, can find its place in the history of art.

All his life he has copied works of the past, hoping thereby to find a path in his search: Egyptian (page 105), Cycladic and African sculpture, the Roman portraits of the Faiyum, and Byzantine mosaics; he has done copies of the work of Cimabue and Giotto, Conrad Witz and Albrecht Dürer, Tintoretto, Rubens and Callot, Corot and Cézanne, as well as of his contemporaries. But he believes, finally, that the task of art has always been insurmountable, that all the achievements of the past were only tentative efforts, and that only his own work can lead him toward a greater understanding of the nature of reality.

The subject, although repetitious, is not a matter of indifference. He depicts his brother and his wife and his intimate environment. The landscapes at Stampa remain the same, as do the interiors and still lifes. The figures, the standing females, hands on hips, who seem to be offering themselves in their elusiveness, the male heads, or walking men, hardly ever vary. They do not have much individuality; nothing, in fact, would interest Giacometti less than a psychological interpretation of the individual. Indeed, the longer a person sits for him, the more unknown, almost terrifying, he becomes. It is the basic structure of the head, not the personality of the sitter, that concerns him, not man's individuality but, rather, his universality. In this respect he recalls his important Swiss predecessor, Ferdinand Hodler, whose "parallelism" was the stylized symbolic expression of human solidarity.

Giacometti is convinced that this expression of universality can be achieved only by means of the most painstaking study of nature. He first modeled a head from nature in 1914 when he was a young boy —a head, he points out, that was the same size as those of his current endeavors. He studied first with his father, the well-known Impressionist painter Giovanni Giacometti, then in Geneva, and finally with Bourdelle in Paris. As he explains in his autobiographical letter (pages 14-29), he soon gave up his hope of being able to work from nature, so he abandoned the model and, about 1925, began working from memory and imagination. For ten years he engaged in a series of highly original experiments. Subject to various influences, primitive and archaic carving as well as then-current Cubist sculpture (the work of Laurens and Lipchitz was of considerable interest to him), he yet affirmed a personality entirely his own. This became apparent as early as 1926 when he exhibited his *Couple* (page 33) at the Salon des Tuileries, at Bourdelle's invitation. These bizarre and amusing monoliths and the monumentally concave *Spoon Woman* (pages 30, 31) combine a powerful plastic confrontation with symbolic erotic content. Of great importance was a series of heads with oval indentations (page 32) which had become flat during the working process without the sculptor's intention. Soon he felt the need of opening his forms and made undulating or static grill-like forms (pages 34, 35), and then open cages where he was able to analyze the object from the inside. Caves and enclosures dominate his memories of childhood— no wonder then that sculpture for him was to become the hollowing out of space. The cages, to which he turned around 1930, reach their climax in the fantastic *Palace at 4 A.M.* (page 45) which was completely realized in his mind in all its absurd precision before it was made.

Constantly searching for new sculptural concepts, he was also interested in the possibilities of obtaining actual kinetic movement and constructed his *Suspended Ball* (page 36) in which a cloven sphere, held by a thread, can be made to slide along a crescent-shaped object. His frank erotic symbolism, the near-abstraction of his work, his exploitation of the dream and reliance on the unconscious, brought him into close contact with the Surrealists, and for a brief time he took part in their exhibitions and wrote for their publications. But whereas they seemed satisfied once they had found a certain style and imagery, Giacometti continued to experiment, discovering new forms and symbols, such as the frightening *Hand Caught by a Finger* (page 37), a fiendish system of gears which, if they did function, would grind the hand to bits. The violent and destructive aspects of his imagination and an obsession with sexual murder is revealed most clearly in the *Woman with Her Throat Cut* (page 38), a nightmarish image, part woman, part animal, part machine. In the *Invisible Object* (page 43), on the other hand, his frightened self and his perpetual fear of the void find a mysterious climax. Simultaneously with work of this Surrealist nature, Giacometti also explored the solidity of objects, making his remarkable *Cubist Head* (page 40), which once again shows his fascination with man's glance.

But all the time he was aware that the day was not far off when he would once more have to sit down before a model and come to grips with the visible world. This became clear to him while he and Diego were engaged in the design and manufacture of vases, lamps, chairs, and tables for a fashionable Paris decorator. He realized that he was working on vases the same way he worked on sculptures, and he decided that a clear distinction had to be made between the manufacture of a fine object and the mystery of sculpture.

He went back to working from life, expecting, as he recalled in his letter to refresh his eyes for two weeks; instead he was to work all day for five years. There was a time when the human form became no bigger than a pin (page 47) and, reduced almost beyond its ultimate minimum, was barely able to withstand the onslaught of the void. Then, slowly, after the war, new figures began to emerge, elongated effigies rooted to their bases with enormous feet, superbly arresting in their immobility.

The reduction that had taken place was not only in the almost ascetic thinness of the figure. The compelling *Hand* of 1947 (page 48) is more powerful in its effect than the caught hand of fifteen years earlier, precisely because it has abandoned all paraphernalia and exists with a mysterious power and contained violence. In the late forties he created unforgettable group compositions, of men passing each other in anxious search of their loneliness (page 56), or standing straight and detached like trees in Alpine forests (page 54), or separated from the viewer by an insurmountable chasm of space (page 60).

In his paintings, which begin again after the war, the problem of distance is also dominant: the repeated framing device isolates the sitter into an environment that is remote and uncertain. These grisaille paintings with their restrained colors seem out of place in a time when our sensibilities are constantly blunted by the brilliance of fresh and garish color. But colors, Giacometti feels, adhere to surfaces, and his problem—the problem of the sculptor as painter—is to grasp the totality of the image in space. His linear painting, nervous mobile drawings, and sculptures of "petrified incompletion" testify to a great artist's struggle to find an equivalent for the human phenomenon.

11

1901    Alberto Giacometti born October 10 in Stampa (Grisons), Switzerland, a small village near the Italian border, to Annetta and Giovanni Giacometti (1868-1933), a well-known Impressionist painter.

1910-    Begins drawing from nature at the age of nine.
1914    Paints his first picture, of apples, in 1913; in 1914 makes his first sculpture, a bust of his younger brother Diego, which he still owns. Uses other members of his family as models.

1915-    Attends secondary school in Schiers (Grisons),
1918    where he is interested in literature (the German Romantics, Goethe, Hölderlin), the natural sciences, and history. Continues to draw, paint, and sculpt.

1919    Takes a three-month leave from school to consider what he wants to do and decides to devote himself to art. Leaves the Ecole des Beaux-Arts in Geneva after three days because he is not permitted to draw what he wishes and enters the Ecole des Arts-et-Métiers where he studies sculpture.

1920-    Accompanies father, commissioner of the Swiss
1921    pavilion at the Biennale, to Venice. Is attracted to the mosaics in San Marco and to Bellini's paintings, forms a passionate love for the works of Tintoretto but is even more impressed by Giotto's frescoes which he sees on a trip to Padua. Visits Florence and Assisi, where he is overwhelmed by Cimabue's paintings; lives in Rome for nine months where he is fascinated by the Egyptian collection in the Vatican museum, admires Baroque art (Borromini) and Early Christian mosaics. Knows the work of the Futurists. Copies many works of art, paints portraits and landscapes. Begins two sculptured busts but for the first time experiences difficulty working from the model and destroys them before leaving Rome.

1922-    Arrives in Paris, January 1, 1922. Enters the
1925    Académie de la Grande-Chaumière, where he stays for three years in Bourdelle's class.

1925-    Takes his first studio, on the rue Froidevaux,
1926    which he shares with his brother Diego. The difficulties experienced in Rome in working from life recur and he begins to work from his imagination—a practice that he will follow almost exclusively for the next 10 years. The first works are of a Cubist nature (*Torso*). Influences from African art, Cycladic sculpture, and the work of Laurens and Lipchitz lead at first to solid, compact structures (*The Couple, The Spoon Woman*) and thin, tablet-like works. Begins to exhibit at the Salon des Tuileries.

1927    Moves into the studio on the rue Hippolyte-Maindron which he still occupies, to which Diego's workrooms are adjacent.

1928    Continues to develop the tablet-like sculptures and begins to make openwork structures (*Three Persons Out Of Doors, Man and Woman*). Meets Tériade, André Masson, and Michel Leiris, who becomes one of his closest friends. Also meets the dissident members of the Surrealist group: Queneau, Limbour, Desnos, Prévert. Knows Miró and Calder.

1929-    Development of the transparent constructions
1930    (*Reclining Woman Who Dreams, Standing Man*). Makes his first "cage" sculpture (*Suspended Ball*). Meets Aragon, Breton, and Dali. Joins the Surrealists and becomes a participant in the group's activities, publications, and exhibitions. To earn their living he and Diego make chandeliers, vases, chairs, and other furnishings for the interior decorator Jean-Michel Frank, which they will continue to do for many years. Exhibits objects with Miró and Arp at the Galerie Pierre.

1931-    Dislikes sculpture that gives an illusion of
1934    movement and begins to make sculptures with movable parts (*Hand Caught by a Finger, No More Play*). The cage sculptures, which had consisted of single units, culminate in the more complex *Palace at 4 A.M.* Dissatisfaction with the objects he has been making begins to lead him away from abstract pieces toward more figurative sculptures, and the 10-year period of working from the imagination ends with such works as *Walking Nude, 1 + 1 = 3, The Invisible Object*, and a series of skull-like heads. Has first one-man show in 1932 in Paris at the Galerie Pierre Colle; participates in the Surrealist exhibition at the Galerie Pierre Colle in 1933; in 1934 has his first one-man show in New York at the Julien Levy Gallery.

1935    Begins to make sculptures from nature again. Is officially expelled from the Surrealist group. From now on will work from both life and imagination, at times adhering to one method or the other for a period, more often following both practices concurrently on different works in hand. Friendships with Balthus, Gruber, and Tal Coat. Frequently sees André Derain whose work interests him enormously. Has 3 works in the exhibition *Thèse-Antithèse-Synthèse* held at the Kunstmuseum, Lucerne.

1936    Has 8 works in the *International Surrealist Exhibition* held in London at the New Burlington Galleries; 3 works in the exhibition *Fantastic Art, Dada, Surrealism* at The Museum of Modern Art, New York.

1938    Is run over by a drunken motorist; spends months in the hospital undergoing painful treatment for his injured foot, while under constant threat of amputation.

1948-
1950  Continues making elongated figures whose bronzed surfaces appear scarred and eroded; begins to paint some of them. Creates a series of skeletal figures in motion (*City Square, Three Men Walking, Walking Quickly Under the Rain*) and of figures located precisely in space (*Chariot, Four Figurines on a Base*). The desire for less rigidity is fulfilled, by accident, by compositions made by grouping a number of figures, each of which had been created independently (*Composition with Seven Figures and a Head*). Major exhibitions at the Pierre Matisse Gallery, New York, in 1948 and 1950; included in group exhibitions in Amsterdam (1948) and Bern (1950); shares a two-man exhibition with André Masson in Basel (1950).

1951  Makes sculptures that are apart from the recurrent themes of standing figures and portrait busts (*Horses* [destroyed], *Dog*). First exhibition at the Galerie Maeght, Paris.

1952-
1953  Makes a series of small, stubby figures in plaster and bronze (*Standing Nude*); elongated figures and busts also become more rounded. Becomes interested in printmaking, especially lithography. Included in group exhibitions in Basel (1952), at The Museum of Modern Art, New York (1952); one-man exhibition of 26 works at the Arts Club, Chicago.

1954-
1955  Commissioned by the French Mint to make a medal of Henri Matisse, he makes many drawings of the aged artist shortly before Matisse's death. Meets Jean Genet. Exhibitions in New York at the Pierre Matisse Gallery and in Paris at Galerie Maeght (1954); large retrospectives held at the Solomon R. Guggenheim Museum, New York, and by the Arts Council of Great Britain in London (1955).

1956  Exhibits a series of monumental female figures at the Biennale, Venice; large one-man show at the Kunsthalle, Bern.

1940-
1942  Abandons working from a model and begins again to work from his imagination, which leads to a series of minuscule figures. Sees Picasso often, becomes friendly with Sartre.

1942-
1945  Lives in Switzerland, primarily Geneva. Meets Annette Arm who will become his wife. Contributes drawings and articles—on Laurens, Callot—to the magazine *Labyrinthe* published by Skira. The problem of the tiny figure continues, and when he leaves Switzerland to return to Paris his entire production of these years is said to fit into 6 matchboxes. One-man show in New York at Peggy Guggenheim's Art of This Century gallery includes 9 earlier works.

1945-
1947  Returns to Paris. The difficulty of the tiny figure is resolved through drawing, and the figures become larger, but now they satisfy him only when they are tall and slender (*Man Pointing*). Begins painting again, from nature: still lifes, landscapes, and especially portraits.

1957-
1961  Monumental figures (*Walking Man I, Tall Figures I-IV*) conceived in connection with an outdoor project (1960). Concentration on elongated figures and busts continues, but surfaces begin to become more fluid, forms more rounded, resulting in more approachable figures (*Monumental Head, Bust of Annette*). His paintings, too, achieve greater realism (*Caroline*). Included in many group exhibitions in Europe and the United States; exhibits fairly regularly at his galleries in Paris and New York; large exhibitions at Galerie Klipstein & Kornfeld, Bern (1959), World House Galleries, New York (1960). Wins sculpture prize at the International Exhibition of Contemporary Painting and Sculpture, Carnegie Institute, Pittsburgh (1961).

1962-
1963  Awarded the grand prize for sculpture at the Biennale, Venice (1962); large retrospective exhibitions at the Museum of Fine Arts, Zurich (1962) and Galerie Beyeler, Basel (1963).

1964  Opening of the Fondation Marguerite et Aimé Maeght in St.-Paul-de-Vence in which his works occupy a prominent place; chandeliers and many furnishings for the museum made by Diego. Announcement of a plan to establish a foundation in Zurich to house and add to a large collection of sculptures, paintings, and drawings. Wins the Guggenheim International Award in an exhibition sponsored by the Solomon R. Guggenheim Museum, New York.

Plaster study for *Tall Figure*. 1960.
Outside the studio.

13

## A LETTER FROM ALBERTO GIACOMETTI
## TO PIERRE MATISSE, 1947

First published in NEW YORK, PIERRE MATISSE GALLERY.
*Exhibition of Sculptures, Paintings, Drawings,*
New York, January 19-February 14, 1948.
Reproduced by permission of Pierre Matisse.

Here is the list of sculptures that I promised you, but I could not make it without including, though very briefly, a certain chain of events, without which it would make no sense.

I made my first bust from life in 1914, and continued during the following years throughout the whole period of my schooling. I still have a certain number of these busts and always look at the first with a certain longing and nostalgia.

At the same time, and for many years before, I was drawing a great deal and painting. In addition to drawing from nature and illustrating the books I read, I often copied paintings and sculptures from reproductions. I mention this because with only short interruptions I have continued to do the same thing up to the present.

In 1919 I went to the Ecole des Beaux-Arts in Geneva for three days, and then to the Ecole des Arts-et-Métiers in the same city to study sculpture. I painted watercolors in the countryside and at the lake shore, and did oil paintings at home.

In 1920-21 I lived in Italy. In Venice first, where I spent my days looking mostly at the Tintorettos, not wanting to miss a single one.

To my great regret, on the day I left Venice, Tintoretto was a little dethroned by the Giottos in Padua, and he in turn some months later by Cimabue at Assisi.

I stayed nine months in Rome where I never had enough time to do all I wanted. I wanted to see everything, and at the same time I painted, figures, somewhat pointillist landscapes (I had become convinced that the sky is blue only by convention and that it is actually red), and compositions inspired by Sophocles and Aes-

Voici la liste des sculptures que je vous ai promise, mais je
ne peux la faire qu'en y introduisant un certain enchaînement, d'ailleurs très sommaire, sans cela elle n'aurait aucun sens.

J'ai fait mon premier buste d'après nature en 1914 et continuais
les années suivantes pendant toute l'époque du collège. Je possède
encore un certain nombre de ces bustes et je regarde toujours le
premier avec une certaine envie et nostalgie.

En même temps et bien des années avant déjà je dessinais beau-
coup et je faisais de la peinture. A côté des dessins d'après
nature et des illustrations de livres que je lisais, je copiais
souvent des tableaux et des sculptures d'après des reproductions.
Je cite ceci parce que j'ai continué la même activité avec de très
courtes interruptions jusqu'à présent.

En 1919 j'étais pendant ~~à peine une année à~~ 3 jours l'Ecole des Beaux-
et après à l'école des Arts et métiers de la même ville pour la sculpture
Arts à Genève. ~~J'avais de l'aversion pour celle-ci~~ et je faisais
~~surtout~~ des aquarelles dans les environs et au bord du lac et de la
peinture chez moi.

En 1920-21 j'ai vécu en Italie. A Venise d'abord où j'ai
passé les journées à regarder les Tintoret surtout, ne voulant pas
qu'il y en ait un seul qui m'échappe.

Tintoret fut un peu détrôné, à ma grande peine, le jour même
où je quittai Venise par les Giotto de Padoue, et celui-ci, à son
tour, quelques mois plus tard, par Cimabue à Assisi.

Je restai neuf mois à Rome où le temps me manqua toujours pour
faire tout ce que je voulais. J'avais envie de tout voir et en même
temps je faisais de la peinture, des figures, des paysages un peu
pointillistes ( j'avais acquis la conviction que le ciel n'est bleu
que par convention mais rouge en réalité ) et des compositions d'après

15

But if, on the other hand, one began by analyzing a detail, the end of the nose, for example, one was lost. One could have spent a lifetime without achieving a result. The form dissolved, it was little more than granules moving over a deep black void, the distance between one wing of the nose and the other is like the Sahara, without end, nothing to fix one's gaze upon, everything escapes.

Since I wanted nevertheless to realize a little of what I saw, I began as a last resort to work at home from memory. I tried to do what I could to avoid this catastrophe. This yielded, after many attempts touching on cubism, one necessarily had to touch on it (it is too long to explain now) objects which were for me the closest I could come to my vision of reality.

This gave me some part of my vision of reality, but I still lacked a sense of the whole, a structure, also a sharpness that I saw, a kind of skeleton in space.

*Ma,* Si par ~~contre~~ ~~malheur~~ on commençait par analyser) *un détail* le bout du nez, par
exemple, on était perdu. On aurait pu y passer la vie sans arriver
à un résultat. La forme se défait, ce n'est plus que comme des
grains qui bougent sur un vide noir et profond, la distance entre
une aile du nez et l'autre est comme le Sahara, pas de limite, rien
à fixer, tout échappe.

Comme je voulais tout de même ~~faire~~ *réaliser un peu* ce que je voyais, j'ai com-
mencé, en désespoir de cause, à travailler chez moi de mémoire. J'ai
tâché de faire le peu que je pouvais sauver de cette catastrophe.
Ceci a donné, après quantité d'essais qui touchaient au cubisme, on
devait forcément y toucher (c'est trop long à expliquer maintenant),
des objets qui étaient pour moi ce que je pouvais faire de plus
proche à ~~la réalité~~. *de ma vision de la réalité,*

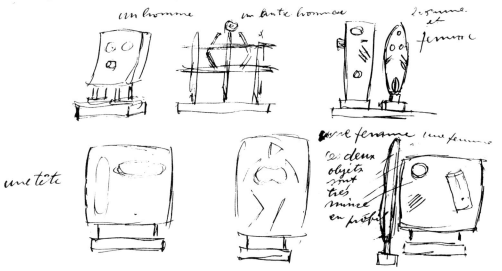

Ceci donnait pour moi une certaine partie de la vision de la
réalité; mais il me manquait ce que je ressentais pour l'ensemble,
une structure, un côté aigu que j'y voyais aussi, une espèce de
squelette dans l'espace.

Figures were never for me a compact mass but like a transparent construction.

Again, after making all kinds of attempts, I made cages with open construction inside, executed in wood by a carpenter.

There was a third element in reality that concerned me: movement.

Despite all my efforts, it was impossible for me then to endure a sculpture that gave an illusion of movement, a leg advancing, a raised arm, a head looking sideways. I could only create such movement if it was real and actual, I also wanted to give the sensation of motion that could be induced.

Several objects which move in relation to one another.

## 4

Les figures n'étaient jamais pour moi une masse compacte, mais comme une construction transparente.

Après de nouveau toute espèce d'essais, j'ai fait des cages avec une construction libre à l'intérieur, exécutées en bois par un menuisier. *très mal dessiné*

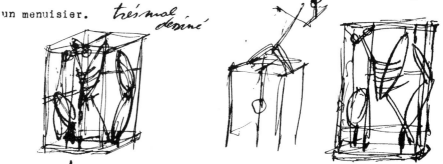

Mais Il y avait un troisième élément qui me touchait dans la réalité: le mouvement.

Malgré tous mes efforts, il m'était alors impossible de supporter une sculpture qui donne l'illusion d'un mouvement, une jambe qui avance, un bras levé, une tête qui regarde de côté. Ce mouvement, je ne pouvais le faire que réel et effectif, je voulais donner aussi la sensation de le provoquer.

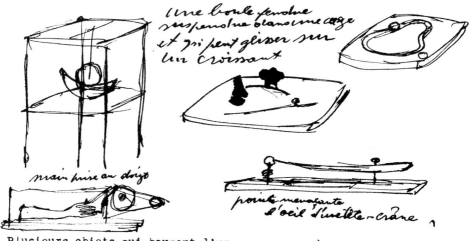

Plusieurs objets qui bougent l'un par rapport à l'autre.

But all this took me away little by little from external reality, I had a tendency to become absorbed only in the construction of the objects themselves.

There was something in these objects that was too precious, too classical; and I was disturbed by reality, which seemed to me to be different. Everything at that moment seemed a little grotesque, without value, to be thrown away.

This is being said too briefly.

Objects without pedestals and without value, to be thrown away.

It was no longer the exterior forms that interested me but what I really felt. (During all the previous years—the period of the academy—there had been for me a disagreeable contrast between life and work, one got in the way of the other, I could find no solution. The fact of wanting to copy a body at set hours and a body to which otherwise I was indifferent, seemed to me an activity that was basically false, stupid, and which made me waste many hours of my life.)

It was no longer a question of reproducing a lifelike figure but of living, and of executing only what had affected me, or what I really wanted. But all this alternated, contradicted itself, and continued by

## 5

Mais tout ceci m'éloignait peu à peu de la réalité extérieure, j'avais tendance à ne me passionner que pour la construction des objets eux-mêmes.

Il y avait dans ces objets un côté trop précieux, trop clas-
sique; et j'étais troublé par la réalité qui me semblait autre.
*dans celle' à ce moment la*
Tout me semblait un peu grotesque, sans valeur, à jeter.

Ceci est dit d'une manière trop sommaire.

Objets sans base et sans valeur, à jeter.

Ce n'était plus la forme extérieure des êtres qui m'intéres-
sait, mais ce que je sentais affectivement dans ma vie. (Pendant
toutes les années précédentes (époque de l'Académie), il y avait
eu pour moi un contraste désagréable entre la vie et le travail,
l'un empêchait l'autre, je ne trouvais pas de solution. Le fait
de vouloir copier un corps à heures fixes, et un corps qui m'était
par ailleurs indifférent, me semblait une activité fausse à sa
base, bête, et qui me faisait perdre des heures de vie ).

Il ne s'agissait plus de présenter une figure extérieurement
ressemblante, mais de vivre et de ne réaliser que ce qui m'avait
affecté, ou que je désirais. Mais tout ceci alternait, se contre-

contrast. There was also a need to find a solution between things that were rounded and calm, and sharp and violent. It is this which led during those years (32-34 approximately) to objects going in directions that were quite different from each other, a kind of landscape —a head lying down; a woman strangled, her jugular vein cut; construction of a palece with a skeleton bird and a spinal column in a cage and a woman at the other end. A model for a large garden sculpture, I wanted people to be able to walk on the sculpture, to sit on it and lean on it. A table for a hall, and very abstract objects which then led me to figures and skull heads.

disait et continuait par contraste. Désir aussi de trouver une

solution entre les choses pleines et calmes et

aiguës et violentes. Ce qui donna *pendant ces années*

*là (32 – 34 a peuprés ) des objets allant dans*

*des directions assez differentes, une de l'autre,*

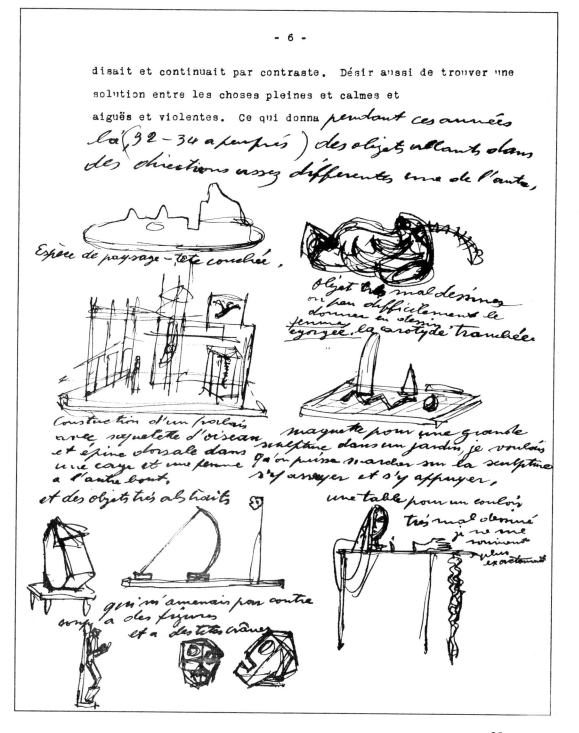

*Espèce de paysage – tête couchée,*

*Objet très mal dessiné*
*on peu difficilement le*
*donner en dessin*
*femme egorgée, la carotyde tranchée*

*Construction d'un palais*
*avec squelette d'oiseau*
*et épine dorsale dans*
*une cage et une femme*
*a l'autre bout,*

*maquette pour une grande*
*sculpture dans un jardin, je voulais*
*qu'on puisse marcher sur la sculpture*
*s'y asseyer et s'y appuyer,*

*et des objets très abstraits*

*une table pour un couloir*
*très mal dessiné*
*je ne me*
*souviens*
*plus exactement*

*qui m'amenais par contre*
*souq a des figures*
*et a des têtes crânes*

I saw anew the bodies that attracted me in reality and the abstract forms which seemed to me true in sculpture, but I wanted to create the former without losing the latter, *very briefly put.*

A last figure, a woman called $1 + 1 = 3$, which I could not resolve.

And then the wish to make compositions with figures. For this, I had to make (quickly I thought; in passing), one or two studies from nature, just enough to understand the construction of a head, of a whole figure, and in 1935 I took a model. This study should take (I thought) two weeks, and then I could realize my compositions.

I worked with the model all day from 1935 to 1940.

Nothing was as I had imagined. A head (I quickly abandoned figures, that would have been too much) became for me an object completely unknown and without dimensions. Twice a year I began two heads, always the same ones, never completing them, and I put my studies aside (I still have the casts).

Finally, in order to accomplish at least a little, I began to work from memory, but this mainly to know what I had gotten out of all this work. (During all these years I drew and painted a little, and almost always from life.)

## 7

Je voyais de nouveau les corps qui m'attiraient dans la réalité et les formes abstraites qui me semblaient vraies en sculpture, mais je voulais faire cela sans perdre ceci *très sommairement oLit*

Une dernière figure, une femme qui s'appelait 1 + 1 = 3

dont je ne me sortais pas.

Et puis le désir de faire des compositions avec des figures. Pour cela il me fallait faire ( vite je croyais, en passant ) une ou deux études d'après nature, juste assez pour comprendre la construction d'une tête, de toute une figure, et, en 1935, je pris un modèle. Cette étude devait me prendre ( je pensais ) une quinzaine de jours, et puis je voulais ~~construire~~ *réaliser* mes compositions.

J'ai travaillé avec modèle toute la journée de 1935 à 1940.

Rien n'était tel que j'imaginais. Une tête ( je laissais de côté *très vite* les figures, ç'en était trop ) devenait pour moi un objet totalement inconnu et sans dimensions. Deux fois par an je commençais deux têtes, toujours les mêmes, sans jamais aboutir, et je mettais mes études à côté ( donc j'ai encore les moules ).

Enfin, pour tâcher de les réaliser un peu, je recommençai à travailler ~~de~~ mémoire) *mais ceci surtout pour* ~~pour~~ savoir ~~surtout~~ ce qui me restait de tout ce travail. (Pendant toutes ces années j'ai dessiné et fait un peu de peinture) *et presque toujours d'après nature,*

But wanting to create from memory what I had seen, to my terror the sculptures became smaller and smaller, they had a likeness only when they were small, yet their dimensions revolted me, and tirelessly I began again, only to end several months later at the same point.

A large figure seemed to me false and a small one equally unbearable, and then often they became so tiny that with one touch of my knife they disappeared into dust. But head and figures seemed to me to have a bit of truth only when small.

All this changed a little in 1945 through drawing.

This led me to want to make larger figures, but then to my surprise, they achieved a likeness only when tall and slender.

And this is almost where I am today, no, where I still was yesterday, and I realize right now that if I can draw ancient sculptures with ease, I could draw those I made during these last years only with difficulty; perhaps if I could draw them it would no longer be necessary to create them in space, but I am not sure about this.

And now I stop, besides they are closing, I must pay.

## 8

Mais voulant faire ~~de~~ mémoire ce que j'avais vu, à ma terreur,
les sculptures devenaient de plus en plus petites, elles n'étaient
ressemblantes que petites, et pourtant ces dimensions me révoltaient
et, inlassablement, je recommençais pour aboutir, après quelques
mois, au même point.

Une grande figure était pour moi fausse et une petite tout
de même intolérable *et puis elles devenez n' ni minuscules que*
*sonnent avec un dernier coup de canif et disparaissant dans*
~~mais~~ Têtes et figures n'étaient un peu vraies que minuscules. *la*
*ne me semblais* *poussière*

*si celle ci* *y peu près*

Tout ceci changea un peu en 1945 par le dessin.
*Ceci m'amena a vouloir* *Plus*
~~Je voulus à tout prix~~ faire des figures grandes, ~~ou au moins~~
~~pas absolument minuscules,~~ mais alors, à ma surprise, elles n'étaient
ressemblantes que longues et minces.

~~Mais aujourd'hui, je ne peux plus les dessiner.~~
*la*
Et ~~puis~~ c'est à peu près où j'en suis aujourd'hui, ~~ou plutôt~~
*non, ou*
~~où~~ j'en étais hier encore, et je m'aperçois à l'instant que si je
*pourrais*
peux facilement dessiner les sculptures anciennes, je ne ~~peux pas~~
*que difficilement* *peut être que si jé*
dessiner celles que j'ai faites les dernières années. ~~Si je~~ pouvais les dessiner, il ne serait plus nécessaire de les faire dans
l'espace *mais je ne suis pas sur de ceci*
*Et*
~~Mais~~ je m'arrête, d'ailleurs on ferme, il faut régler.

opposite: *The Spoon Woman.* 1926. Plaster, 47¼" high.

below: *The Spoon Woman.* 1926. Bronze, 57¼" high. Collection Mr. and Mrs. Arnold H. Maremont.

Torso. 1925. Bronze, 22½" high. Museum of Fine Arts, Zurich.
(Cast in exhibition, Collection Mr. and Mrs. Arnold H. Maremont)

31

left: *The Artist's Mother*. 1927. Plaster, 11¾" high.

below: *Head*. 1928. Bronze, 15⅜" high. The Florene May Schoenborn and Samuel A. Marx Collection.

opposite: *The Couple*. 1926. Bronze, 23½" high. Museum of Fine Arts, Zurich.
(Cast in exhibition, Collection Mr. and Mrs. Harry Lewis Winston)

*Man.* 1929. Bronze, 15¾″ high. Collection Dr. and Mrs. Frank Stanton.

34

*. . . I began as a last resort to work at home from memory. . . . This yielded . . . objects*
*which were for me the closest I could come to my vision of reality . . . .*
*a structure, also a sharpness that I saw, a kind of skeleton in space. Figures*
*were never for me a compact mass but like a transparent construction.*

*Reclining Woman Who Dreams.* 1929. Painted bronze, 15⅝″ long. The Joseph H. Hirshhorn Collection.

*Despite all my efforts, it was impossible for me then to endure a sculpture
that gave an illusion of movement, a leg advancing, a raised arm,
a head looking sideways. I could only create such movement if it were real
and actual. I also wanted to give the sensation of motion that could be induced.*

*Suspended Ball.* 1930-31. Wood and metal, 23⅜″ high. Private collection.

*Objects without pedestals and without value, to be thrown away.*

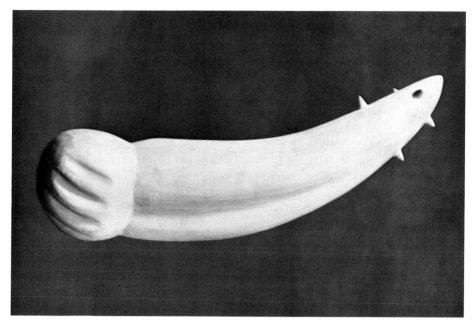

*Disagreeable Object.* 1931. Wood, 19″ long. Collection **Mr.** and Mrs. James Johnson Swenney.

*Several objects which move in relation to one another.*

*Hand Caught by a Finger (Main prise).* 1932. Wood and metal, 23″ long. Museum of Fine Arts, Zurich.

*It was no longer a question of reproducing a lifelike figure but of living,*
*and of executing only what had affected me, or what I really wanted.*
*But all this alternated, contradicted itself, and continued to conflict. There was also*
*a need to find a solution between things that were rounded and calm, and sharp and violent.*
*It is this which led during those years ( 32-34 approximately ) to*
*objects going in directions*
*that were quite different from each other .... a woman strangled, her jugular vein cut ....*

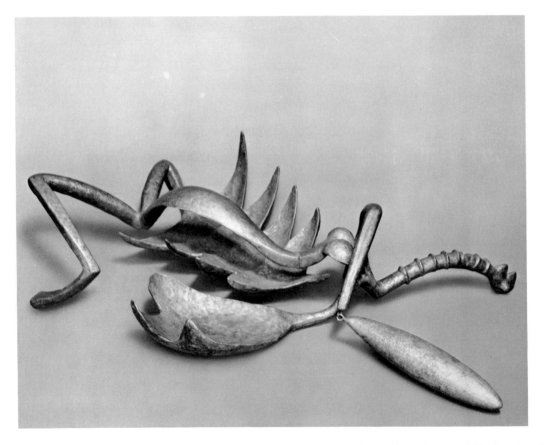

*Woman with Her Throat Cut (Femme égorgée).* 1932. **Bronze,** 34½″ long. The Museum of Modern Art, N.Y.

*No More Play*. 1933. Marble, wood, bronze, 23 x 17⅝". Collection Mr. and Mrs. Julien Levy.

opposite: *Tall Figure, Half-Size.* 1947. Bronze, 52″ high. The Florene May Schoenborn and Samuel A. Marx Collection.

*I could have destroyed it. But I made this statue for just the opposite reason—to renew myself. Perhaps this is what makes it worthwhile.*

*Nude (Femme qui marche).* 1933-34. Bronze, 59″ high. Museum of Fine Arts, Boston.

*Invisible Object (Hands Holding the Void)* 1934-35. Bronze, 61″ high. Collection Mr. and Mrs. Lee A. Ault.

43

*This object took shape little by little in the late summer of 1932; it revealed
itself to me slowly, the various parts taking their exact form and their
precise place within the whole. By autumn it had attained such reality that
its actual execution in space took no more than one day.
It is related without any doubt to a period in my life that had come to an end
a year before, when for six whole months hour after hour was passed
in the company of a woman who, concentrating all life in herself, magically
transformed my every moment. We used to construct a fantastic palace at night
—days and nights had the same color, as if everything
happened just before daybreak; throughout the whole time I never saw the sun—
a very fragile palace of matchsticks.
At the slightest false move a whole section of this tiny construction would collapse.
We would always begin it over again.
I don't know why it came to be inhabited by a spinal column in a cage
—the spinal column this woman sold me one of the very first nights I met her
on the street—and by one of the skeleton birds that she saw
the very night before the morning in which our life together collapsed—
the skeleton birds that flutter with cries of joy at four o'clock
in the morning very high above the pool of clear, green water where the extremely
fine, white skeletons of fish float in the great unroofed hall.
In the middle there rises the scaffolding of a tower, perhaps unfinished or,
since its top has collapsed, perhaps also broken.
On the other side there appeared the statue of a woman, in which I recognize
my mother, just as she appears in my earliest memories. The mystery of her long
black dress touching the floor troubled me;
it seemed to me like a part of her body, and aroused in me a feeling of
fear and confusion. All the rest has vanished, and escaped my attention. This
figure stands out against the curtain that is repeated three times,
the very curtain I saw when I opened my eyes for the first time . . . .
I can't say anything about the red object in front of the board;
I identify it with myself.*

*The Palace at 4 A.M.* 1932-33. Wood, glass, wire, string, 25" high. The Museum of Modern Art, New York.

*Woman with the Chariot I.* 1942-43. Bronze, 61¾" high. Pierre Matisse Gallery, New York.

*... I began to work from memory again .... to my terror the
sculptures became smaller and smaller, they had a likeness only
when they were very small, yet their dimensions revolted me, and
tirelessly I began again, only to end several months later
at the same point.
A large figure seemed to me false and a small one equally unbearable,
and then often they became so tiny that with
one touch of my knife they disappeared into dust. But head and
figures seemed to me to have a bit of truth only when small.*

*Figurines.* c. 1945. Plaster over metal. Left, 4⅜" high; right, 3⅜" high, including
plaster bases. Collection Mr. and Mrs. Thomas B. Hess.

*Man Pointing.* 1947. Bronze, 70½″ high. The Museum of Modern Art, New York. Gift of Mrs. John D. Rockefeller, 3rd.

*Hand.* 1947. Bronze, 28¼″ long. Collection Mr. and Mrs. Paul Peralta-Ramos.

page 52: *Head of Diego.* 1954. Bronze, 13¼″ high. Collection Mr. and Mrs. Charles Zadok.

page 53: *Bust of Diego.* 1957. (Detail). Bronze, 24½″ high. The Joseph H. Hirshhorn Collection.

opposite: *Head of a Man on a Rod.* 1947. Bronze and plaster, 21¾″ high. Collection Mr. and Mrs. William N. Eisendrath, Jr.

below: *Head of a Man on a Rod.* 1947. Bronze, 24″ high. Collection Mrs. George Acheson.

*Three Men Walking.* 1949. Bronze, 28¼" high. Private collection, Paris.
(Cast in exhibition, Collection Mr. and Mrs. Burt Kleiner)

*Composition with Seven Figures and a Head (The Forest).* 1950. Painted bronze, 22" high.
The Reader's Digest Association.

*The . . . seven figures one head . . . was also done by chance, as if involuntarily I*
*came to realize impressions felt long before and which I saw in the sculpture*
*only when done . . . . I saw again a precise location where the head takes the form of*
*a stone, there are blocks of granite isolated among the trees, but*
*I dreamed of doing these same heads almost twenty years ago . . . .*
*The composition with seven figures reminded me*
*of a forest corner seen for many years (that was during my childhood) and where*
*trees—behind which could be seen granite boulders—with their naked and slender trunks,*
*limbless almost to the top, had always appeared to me like personages*
*immobilizd in the course of their wanderings and talking among themselves.*

*. . . a street during the rain and the figure was me. . . .*
*Me scurrying down a street in the rain.*

*Walking Quickly under the Rain.* 1949. Bronze, 32″ long. Collection Mr. and Mrs. Gordon Bunshaft.

*City Square.* 1948. Bronze, 8½″ high, 25⅜″ long. The Museum of Modern Art, New York.

56

*A small figure in a box between two boxes that are houses.*

*Between Two Houses.* 1950. Bronze and glass, 20″ long. Private collection, Paris.
(Cast in exhibition, Collection Mr. and Mrs. Stanley Marcus)

*I see this room, I even see the curtains beside the women
(which is still not exactly the effect I wanted)
.... at the same time it's another problem, the desire
to abolish the base, trying to have a limited space to further
realize a head and a figure ....
I saw this composition in its form and color before I started
it, but the figure had raised arms and open hands.
This quickly became unbearable....*

*The Cage.* 1950-51. Bronze, 67″ high. Collection Aimé Maeght.

opposite: *The Cage.* Painted bronze. (Detail).

58

*Several nude women seen at the Sphinx while I was*
*seated at the end of the room.*
*The distance that separated us (the polished floor),*
*which seemed impassable despite my desire*
*to cross it, impressed me as much as the women did.*

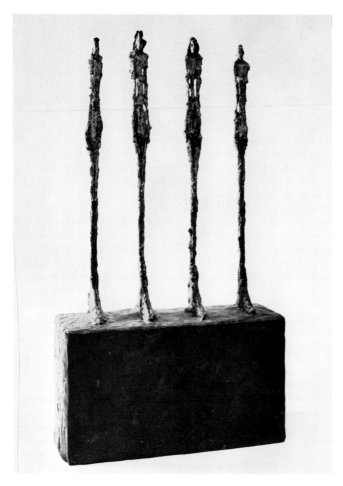

*Four Women on a Base.* 1950. Painted bronze, 31″ high. Museum of
Art, Carnegie Institute, Pittsburgh.

*I could also name the* Chariot *"The Pharmacy Wagon," because this sculpture comes from*
*the glittering wagon that was wheeled around the rooms of the Bichat hospital,*
*which astonished me in 1938.... In 1947 I saw the sculpture before me as if it were finished,*
*and in 1950 it became impossible for me not to make it, even though for me*
*it was already in the past*
*(this is not the only thing that prompted me to make this sculpture).*
*... The* Chariot *was created by the necessity again to have the figure in empty space*
*in order to see it better and to situate it at a precise distance from the floor.*

*Chariot.* 1950. Bronze, 57″ high. The Museum of Modern Art, New York.

*It's me. One day I saw myself in the street just like that. I was the dog.*

*Dog.* 1951. Bronze, 18″ high. The Museum of Modern Art, New York. A. Conger Goodyear Fund.

*Woman, Shoulder Broken (Femme, épaule cassée).* 1958-59. Bronze, 27½″ high.   Collection
Dr. and Mrs. Leo Chalfen.

**63**

*Bust of Annette IV*. 1962. Bronze, 22½″ high. Collection Sylvan and Mary Lang.

*Bust of Diego.* 1955. Plaster, 7½″ high. Collection
Mr. and Mrs. James W. Alsdorf.

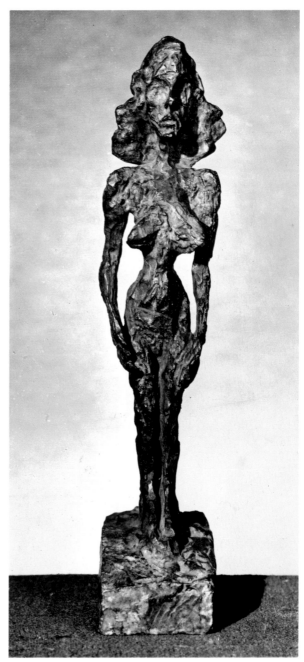

*Standing Nude.* 1953. Painted plaster, 8¾″ high.
Private collection.

*Woman.* 1953. Bronze, 19¼″ high. The Joseph H. Hirshhorn
Collection.

65

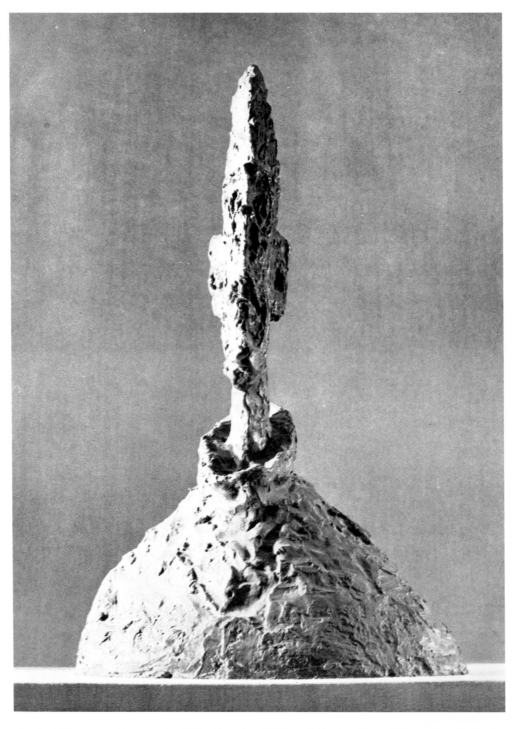

*Head of Diego*. 1954. Bronze, 26½″ high. (Casts in exhibition, Collection Mr. and Mrs. Sidney F. Brody;
Mr. and Mrs. Richard K. Weid)

pages 68-69: *Nine Standing Figures (Venice)*. 1956. Average height 45″. Pierre Matisse Gallery.
left to right: Numbers 2, 4, 6, 9, 7, 1, 8, 3, 5.

*Head*. 1952. Bronze, 15″ high. Collection Aimé Maeght.

*Leg.* 1958-59. Bronze, 7′ high., Pierre Matisse Gallery.

opposite left: *Head of Diego on Stele I.* 1958. Bronze, 63½″ high. Pierre Matisse Gallery.

opposite right: *Head of Diego on Stele III.* 1959. Bronze, 65⅜″ high. (Cast in exhibition, Collection Aimé Maeght)

71

*Tall Figures*. 1960. Bronze. left to right: *Number I*, 8'10¼", Pierre Matisse Gallery; *Number III*, 7'9", Collection Mr. and Mrs. Gordon Bunshaft; *Number II*, 8'1½", Private collection; *Number IV*, 8'10½", Pierre Matisse Gallery.

*Walking Man 1*. 1960. Bronze, 71¾" high. Museum of Art, Carnegie Institute, Pittsburgh.

*Monumental Head.* 1960. Bronze, 37½″ high. The Joseph H. Hirshhorn Collection.

*Bust of Annette.* 1962. Painted bronze, 18½″ high. Private collection.

*Figure   Standing*(13). 1964. Bronze, 26½″ high. Pierre Matisse Gallery.

*Diego at Stampa.* 1921. Oil, 24¾ x 19⅝″. Owned by the artist.

*Self-Portrait.* (1921). Oil, 32½ x 27½". Museum of Fine Arts, Zurich.

*Seated Man.* 1949. Oil, 30¾ x 14½". Collection Mr. and Mrs. Morton
G. Neumann.

*Seated Figure in Studio*. (1950). Oil, 39½ x 31⅞″. Collection Julian J. and Joachim Jean Aberbach.

*The Artist's Mother.* 1950. Oil, 35⅜ x 24″. The Museum of Modern Art, New York. Acquired through the Lillie P. Bliss Bequest.

*The Artist's Mother.* (1937). Oil, 23½″ x 19⅝″. Collection Mrs. Pierre Matisse.

*The Artist's Mother.* (1951). Oil, 36¼ x 28¾". Collection Aimé Maeght.

*The Studio.* 1950. Oil, 25 ¾ x 18¼″. Collection Mr. and Mrs. James W. Alsdorf.

*Scene from Studio Window.* 1950. Oil, 21¼ x 13¼″. Collection Mr. and Mrs. James W. Alsdorf.

*Landscape.* 1952. Oil, 18 x 20″. Collection Mr. and Mrs. Harry W. Sherwood.

*Study of Heads.* 1954. Oil, 31⅞ x 23⅝″. Collection Louis Clayeux.

*Figure.* (1951). Oil, 43¼ x 20½″. Collection Mr. and Mrs. Joseph Bissett.

Study after the *City Square*. 1951. Oil, 24 x 19¾″. Collection Mr. and Mrs. Andrew C. Ritchie.

*Annette.* (1954). Oil, 25½ x 21″. Collection Mr. and Mrs. Arnold H. Maremont.

*Annette.* (1961). Oil, 45¾ x 35″. Collection Mr. and Mrs. Jacques Gelman.

*Sideboard (Le Buffet)*. 1957. Oil, 19¾ x 24″. Collection Mr. and Mrs. Joseph L. Tucker.

*Caroline*. 1961. Oil, 45¾″ x 35″. Frank and Ursula Laurens Collection.

*Head of a Man.* (1961). Oil, 19 x 16″. Collection Mr. and Mrs. Sidney L. Solomon.

*Head.* (1962). Oil, 36¼ x 28¾". Collection Aimé Maeght.

*Portrait of Simon Bérard.* (c.1918). Pen and ink,
12¼ x 9¼". Collection James Lord.

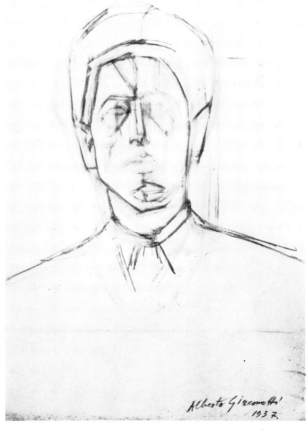

*Self-Portrait.* 1937. Pencil, 19¼ x 12¼". Collection Pierre
Matisse.

94

*Head of a Woman.* 1946. Crayon, 19½ x 13¾". Private collection.

*Standing Nude.* (1947). Oil on paper, 24¾ x 13½″. Collection Eleanor Ward.

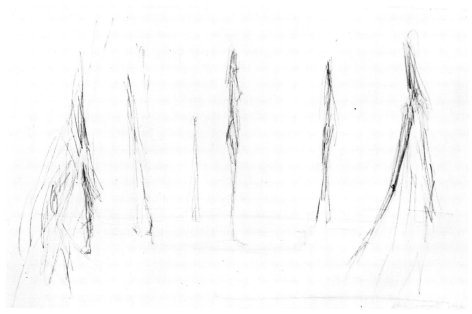

*Figures on City Square.* 1947. Pencil, 12⅞ x 20″. Collection Gene R. Summers.

96

*Walking Man.* (c.1950). Oil on paper, 26¾ x 20″. Collection James Lord.

*Annette in the Studio.* 1956. Pen and ink, 14 x 9½". Collection Mr. and Mrs. James W. Alsdorf.

*Bust on Sculpture Stand.* 1951. Crayon, 22 x 14⅝". Collection Ruth and Hermann Vollmer.

*The Dormer Window.* 1957. Pencil, 25⅝ x 19¾".
Courtesy The Museum of Modern Art.

*Interior.* 1951. Pencil, 14½ x 10¼". Private collection.

*Vase of Flowers.* 1959. Pencil, 19⅜ x 12⅝". Private collection.

*Bottles.* 1956. Oil, 25½ x 21¼". Collection William Inge.

*Portrait of David Sylvester.* 1960. Oil, 45¾ x 35″. Collection Mr. and Mrs. Joseph Pulitzer, Jr.

*Annette.* 1961. Oil, 21⅛ x 17¾″. The Joseph H. Hirshhorn Collection.

*Jean-Paul Sartre.* 1949. Pencil, 11½ x 8⅞″. Collection Ruth and Hermann Vollmer.

*Henri Matisse—Nice.* 1954. Pencil, 18½ x 12⅜″. Collection Alberto Giacometti.

*Igor Stravinsky.* 1957. Pencil, 15⅞ x 11 15/16″. Collection
Mr. and Mrs. Robert D. Graff.

*Self-Portrait* (1955). 19¼ x 12½″. Private collection.

*Tree.* 1952. Pencil, 20 x 13½". Collection Mr. and Mrs. James W. Alsdorf.

opposite: *Mountain.* 1957. Pencil, 19¾ x 25¾". The Solomon R. Guggenheim Museum, New York.

108

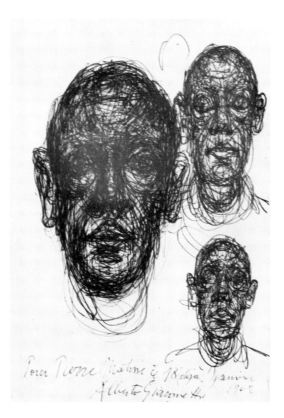

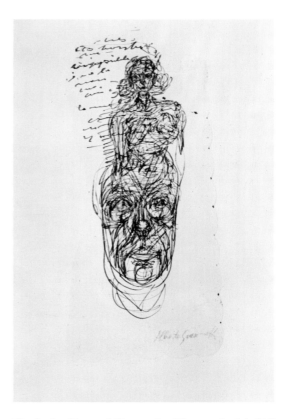

*Three Heads.* 1962. Ball point pen, 8⅛ x 6″.
Collection Pierre Matisse.

*Head of a Man and Torso of a Woman.* (1962). Ball
point pen on paper napkin, 9¾ x 4¾″, irregular. Collection Ruth and Hermann Vollmer.

*Self-Portrait.* (1962). Ball point pen on paper napkin, 7¼ x 5″, irregular. Collection Ruth and Hermann Vollmer.

111

# SELECTED BIBLIOGRAPHY

A comprehensive bibliography compiled by Inga Forslund, Reference Librarian at The Museum of Modern Art, is available in the Library of the Museum. The items listed below represent a selection from that larger work.

## WRITINGS AND STATEMENTS BY GIACOMETTI
*(arranged chronologically)*

Objets mobiles et muets. *Le Surréalisme au service de la révolution* no. 3:18-19, December 1931.

Charbon d'herbe; Poème en 7 espaces; Le Rideau brun. *Le Surréalisme au service de la révolution* no. 5:15, May 1933.

Hier, sables mouvants. *Le Surréalisme au service de la révolution* no. 5:44-45, May 1933.

[Answer to] Enquête [sur la rencontre] d'André Breton, Paul Eluard. *Minotaure* no. 3/4:109, December 1933.

[Notes on the Palace at 4 A.M.]. *Minotaure* no. 3/4:46, December 1933.
   Published in English translation as "1 + 1 = 3," in *Trans/formation* (New York) v. 1, no. 3:165-66, 1952.

Dialogue: André Breton et Alberto Giacometti. *Documents* (Brussels), n.s. no. 1:25, June 1934.

Henri Laurens: Un sculpteur vu par un sculpteur. *Labyrinthe* no. 4:3, January 15, 1945.

A propos de Jacques Callot. *Labyrinthe* no. 7:3, April 15, 1945.

Le Rêve, le sphinx et la mort de T. *Labyrinthe* no. 22:12-13, December 23, 1946.

[Letter to Pierre Matisse]. *In* NEW YORK, PIERRE MATISSE GALLERY. Alberto Giacometti, Exhibition of sculptures, paintings, drawings. January 19-February 14, 1948.

[Letter to Pierre Matisse]. *In* NEW YORK, PIERRE MATISSE GALLERY. Alberto Giacometti. November 1950.

Témoignages. [L'espace]. *XXe siècle* n.s. no. 2:71-72, January 1952.
   Giacometti's answer to an inquiry regarding space, partly in form of a poem.

Gris, brun, noir. *Derrière le miroir.* no. 48/49:2-3, 6-7, June-July 1952.
   On Braque.

Mai 1920. *Verve* v. 7, no. 27/28:33-34, January 15, 1953.
   Drawings by Giacometti after Cimabue and Cézanne.

Derain. *Derrière le miroir* no. 94/95:7-10, February-March 1957.

A chacun sa réalité. *XXe siècle* n.s. no. 9:35, June 1957.
   Giacometti's answer to an inquiry by Pierre Volboudt.

Alberto Giacometti. Schriften, Fotos, Zeichnungen; Essais, photos, dessins. Ed. Ernst Scheidegger. Zurich, Peter Schifferli Verlags AG, 1958.
   Includes: Ma Réalité — L'Espace — Poème en 7 espaces — Le Rideau brun — Charbon d'herbe — Hier, sables mouvants — Lettre à Pierre Matisse — Le Rêve, le sphinx et la mort de T. — Giacometti's catalogue of his early works — Gris, brun, noir. Most of the texts are translated into German. Includes photographs, drawings, chronology.

Entretien avec Alberto Giacometti. *In* CHARBONNIER, GEORGES. Le monologue du peintre. Paris, Juillard, 1959, pp. 159-83.

[Statements]. *In* SELZ, PETER. New Images of Man. New York, The Museum of Modern Art, 1959, p. 68.

Conversation with Giacometti. *Art in America* no. 4:100-2, 1960.
   Interview by Alexander Watt.

Ma longue marche. *L'Express* (Paris), no. 521:48, June 8, 1961.
   Interview by Pierre Schneider.

Pourquoi je suis sculpteur. *Arts* (Paris) no. 873:1, June 13-19, 1962.
   Interview by André Parinaud.

Au Louvre avec Alberto Giacometti. *Preuves* (Paris), no. 139:23-30, September 1962.
   Interview by Pierre Schneider.

## MONOGRAPHS

BUCARELLI, PALMA. Giacometti. Rome, Editalia, 1962.
   Text in Italian, French, and English.

DUPIN, JACQUES. Alberto Giacometti. Paris, Maeght, 1962.
   Published also in an edition with an interleaved English translation by John Ashbery. — The most authoritative and comprehensive monograph in both text and illustrations published so far.

JEDLICKA, GOTTHARD. Alberto Giacometti als Zeichner. Olten, 1960.

MOULIN, RAOUL-JEAN. Giacometti Sculptures (Petite Encyclopédie de l'art, 62). New York, 1964.
   Translated from the French by Bettina Wadia.

YANAIHARA, ISAKU. Giacometti. Tokyo, 1958.

## GENERAL WORKS

BARR, ALFRED H., JR. (ed.). Fantastic Art, Dada, Surrealism. New York, The Museum of Modern Art, 1936; 2nd ed. 1937; 3rd ed. 1946.

BRETON, ANDRÉ. L'Amour fou. Paris, Gallimard, 1937.

CHAR, RENÉ. Recherche de la base et du sommet suivi de pauvreté et privilège. Paris, Gallimard, 1955.

*Derrière le miroir*. Paris, Maeght, October 1956.
Special issue: 10 Ans d'édition.

GIEDION-WELCKER, CAROLA. Contemporary Sculpture. An Evolution in Volume and Space. New York, Wittenborn, 1960.
Enlarged and revised edition of the author's *Modern Plastic Art*, Zurich, Girsberger, 1937.

HOFMANN, WERNER. Die Plastik des 20. Jahrhunderts. Frankfurt am Main, Fischer, 1958.

JORAY, MARCEL. La Sculpture moderne en Suisse (L'Art suisse contemporain, 12, 14). Neuchâtel, Editions du Griffon, 1955-59.
Also published in German.

PIATTE, HANS. Plastik (Die Kunst des 20. Jahrhunderts). Munich, Piper, 1957.

READ, HERBERT. The Art of Sculpture (Bollingen Series, XXXV, 3). New York, Pantheon, 1956.

READ, HERBERT. A Concise History of Modern Sculpture. New York, Praeger, 1964.

RITCHIE, ANDREW CARNDUFF. Sulpture of the Twentieth Century. New York, The Museum of Modern Art, 1952.

SELZ, PETER. New Images of Man. New York, The Museum of Modern Art, 1959.

SEUPHOR, MICHEL. The Sculpture of This Century. New York, Braziller, 1960.
Translation of French ed., *La Sculpture de ce siècle*, Neuchâtel, Editions du Griffon, 1959.

TRIER, EDUARD. Moderne Plastik von Auguste Rodin bis Marino Marini. Berlin, Gebrüder Mann, 1954.

ARTICLES

ASHTON, DORE. Alberto Giacometti. *Arts & Architecture* v. 75, no. 7:10, 31, July 1958.
On the occasion of the exhibition at the Pierre Matisse Gallery.

ASHTON, DORE. New Images of Man. *Arts & Architecture* v. 76, no. 11:14, 15, 40, November 1959.
On the occasion of the exhibition at The Museum of Modern Art.

BRETON, ANDRÉ. Equation de l'objet trouvé. *Documents* (Brussels) n.s. no. 1:17-24, June 1934.

CLAY, JEAN. Giacometti's Dialogue with Death. *Réalités* no. 161:54-59, 76, April 1964.

COURTOIS, MICHEL. La Figuration magique de Giacometti. *Art International* v. 6, no. 5/6:38-45, Summer 1962.

C[URJEL], H[ANS]. Alberto Giacometti. *Werk* v. 50, no. 1:sup. 14-15, January 1963.
On the occasion of the exhibition at the Kunsthaus, Zurich.

C[URJEL], H[ANS]. Eine Alberto Giacometti-Stiftung. *Werk* v. 51, no. 4:sup. 80, April 1964.
The proposal of a Giacometti Foundation at the opening of the exhibition in Landolt-Haus, Zurich, 1964.

D[REXLER], A[RTHUR]. Giacometti, A Change of Space. *Interiors* v. 109, no. 3:102-7, October 1949.

G[ASSER], M[ANUEL] (ed.). Alberto Giacometti. *Du* v. 22, no. 252:2-46, February 1962.
Includes: Vorwort, by Manuel Gasser — Alberto Giacometti also Nachbar, by Herta Wescher — Alberto Giacometti in Genf 1942-1945, by Albert Skira — Jugenderinnerungen an die Familie Giacometti, by Christoph Bernoulli — Ein Gespräch in Maloja, by Carola Giedion-Welcker — Aus einem Tagebuch, by Isaku Yanaihara — Alberto Giacometti und die Wirklichkeit, by Manuel Gasser — Photographs by Franco Gianetti. — Summary in English.

GENET, JEAN. L'Atelier d'Alberto Giacometti. *Derrière le miroir* no. 98, June 1957.
Entire issue devoted to Giacometti. — Published as a book, Décines (Isère), 1963, and in German translation, Zurich, Scheidegger, 1962.

GIEDION-WELCKER, CAROLA. Alberto Giacomettis Vision der Realität. *Werk* v. 46, no. 6:205-12, June 1959.

GIEDION-WELCKER, CAROLA. New Roads in Modern Sculpture. *Transition* no. 23:198-201, July 1935.
Translated from the German.

GREENBERG, CLEMENT. Giacometti. *Nation* v. 166, no. 6:163-64, February 7, 1948.
On the occasion of the exhibition at the Pierre Matisse Gallery.

HABASQUE, GUY. La XXXIe Biennale de Venise. *L'OEil* no. 93:32-41, 72-73, September 1962.

HESS, THOMAS. Giacometti: The Uses of Adversity. *Art News* v. 57, no. 3:34-35, 67, May 1958.

JOUFFROY, ALAIN. Portrait d'un artiste (8): Giacometti. *Arts* (Paris), no. 545:9, December 7-13, 1955.

KRAMER, HILTON. Reappraisals. Giacometti. *Arts* v. 38, no. 2:52-59, November 1963.

LANES, JERROLD. Alberto Giacometti. *Arts Yearbook* 3:152-55, 1959.

LECLERCQ, LENA. Jamais d'espaces imaginaires. *Derrière le miroir* no. 127:6-16, May 1961.

LEIRIS, MICHEL. Alberto Giacometti. *Documents* (Paris), no. 4:209-14, September 1929.

LEIRIS, MICHEL. Alberto Giacometti en timbre-poste ou en médaillon. *L'Arc* v. 5, no. 20:10-13, October 1962.

Published in Italian translation in *La Biennale di Venezia* v. 13, no. 48:10-13, March 1963.

LEIRIS, MICHEL. Pierres pour un Alberto Giacometti. *Derrière le miroir*, no. 29/30, June-July 1951.

Entire issue devoted to Giacometti; served as catalogue to exhibition held at Galerie Maeght, Paris. — A preliminary draft of the text by Leiris was translated into English by Douglas Cooper and published as "Thoughts Around Alberto Giacometti," in *Horizon* v. 19, no. 114:411-17, June 1949.

LIBERMAN, ALEXANDER. Giacometti. *Vogue* (New York) v. 125:146-51, 178-79, January 1955.

LIMBOUR, GEORGES. Giacometti. *Magazine of Art* v. 41, no. 7:253-55, November 1948.

LORD, JAMES. Alberto Giacometti and His Drawings. Introduction to the catalogue of the exhibition at the Pierre Matisse Gallery, New York, 1964.

LORD, JAMES. Alberto Giacometti, sculpteur et peintre. *L'OEil* no. 1:14-20, January 15, 1955.

Published in English in *The Selective Eye*, New York, Random House, 1955.

MALDINEY, HENRI. La Fondation Marguérite et Aimé Maeght. *Derrière le miroir*, no. 148, July 1964.

Issue includes an original lithograph by Giacometti and drawings.

PONGE, FRANCIS. Réflections sur les statuettes, figures & peintures d'Alberto Giacometti. *Cahiers d'art* v. 26:74-90, 1951.

RUSSOLI, FRANCO. Artisti alla Biennale: Alberto Giacometti. *Comunità* v. 10, no. 42:74-77, September 1956.

SARTRE, JEAN-PAUL. Les Peintures de Giacometti. *Derrière le miroir* no. 65, May 1954.

Reprinted in *Les Temps modernes* v. 9 no. 103: 2221-32, June 1954. — Published in English translation by Lionel Abel as "Giacometti in Search of Space," *Art News* v. 54, no. 5:26-29, 63-65, September 1955, and by Warren Ramsey as "The Paintings of Giacometti," in *Art & Artist*, Berkeley and Los Angeles, University of California Press, 1956, pp. 179-94.

SARTE, JEAN-PAUL. Le Recherche de l'absolu. *Les Temps modernes* v. 3, no 28:1153-63, January 1948.

Published in English translation as "The Search for the Absolute" as the introduction to the catalogue of the exhibition at the Pierre Matisse Gallery, 1948.

S[KIRA], A[LBERT]. Alberto Giacometti: Copies d'après un bas-relief égyptien — Conrad Witz — André Derain — Une figure grecque. *Labyrinthe* no. 10:2, July 15, 1945.

SOBY, JAMES THRALL. Alberto Giacometti. *Saturday Review* v. 38, no. 32:36-37, August 6, 1955.

STAHLY, FRANCOIS. Der Bildhauer Alberto Giacometti. *Werk* v. 37, no. 6:181-85, June 1950.

SYLVESTER, DAVID. Perpetuating the Transient. Introduction to the catalogue of the Giacometti exhibition organized by the Arts Council of Great Britain, London, June 4-July 9, 1955.

TARDIEU, JEAN. Giacometti et la solitude. *XXe siècle* n.s. v. 24, no. 18:13-19, February 1962.

WALDBERG, PATRICK. Alberto Giacometti. L'Espace et l'angoisse. *Critique* v. 15, no. 143:329-40, April 1959.

WATT, ALEXANDER. Alberto Giacometti: Pursuit of the Unapproachable. *Studio* v. 167, no. 849:20-27, January 1964.

WESCHER, HERTA. Giacometti: A Profile. *Art Digest* v. 28, no. 5:17, 28-29, December 1, 1953.

WILBUR, RICHARD. Giacometti [Poem]. *Tiger's Eye* no. 7:61-63, March 1949.

Reprinted from Wilbur's *Ceremony and Other Poems*, New York, Harcourt, Brace & Co., 1948.

YANAIHARA, ISAKU. Pages de journal. *Derrière le miroir* no. 127:18-26, May 1961.

Translated from the Japanese. — Published in German translation as "Aus einem Tagebuch," in *Du*, v. 22, no. 252:29-30, February 1962.

ZERVOS, CHRISTIAN. Quelques notes sur les sculptures de Giacometti. *Cahiers d'art*, v. 7, no. 8/10:337-42, 1932.

## CATALOGUE OF THE EXHIBITION

Dimensions are in inches, height preceding width. Dates of the sculpture imply the original conception, in plaster or other materials. In many cases bronze casts were not made the same year. In paintings and drawings, dates enclosed in parentheses do not appear on the works. Works to be shown at only one, two or three museums are marked by (NY), (C), (LA), or (SF) to indicate New York, Chicago, Los Angeles, or San Francisco. Illustrated works are marked with an asterisk.

### SCHEDULE OF THE EXHIBITION

The Museum of Modern Art, New York:
June 9-October 10, 1965

The Art Institute of Chicago:
November 5-December 12, 1965

Los Angeles County Museum of Art:
January 11-February 20, 1966

San Francisco Museum of Art:
March 10-April 24, 1966

### SCULPTURE

*1 *Torso.* 1925. Bronze, 22½" high. Collection Mr. and Mrs. Arnold H. Maremont. Ill. p. 31

*2 *The Couple.* 1926. Bronze, 23½" high. Collection Mr. and Mrs. Harry Lewis Winston. Ill. p. 32

*3 *The Spoon Woman.* 1926. Bronze, 57¼" high. Collection Mr. and Mrs. Arnold H. Maremont. Ill. p. 31

*4 *Head.* 1928. Bronze, 15⅜" high. The Florene May Schoenborn and Samuel A. Marx Collection. Ill. p. 32

*5 *Man.* 1929. Bronze, 15¾" high. Collection Dr. and Mrs. Frank Stanton. Ill. p. 34

*6 *Reclining Woman Who Dreams.* 1929. Painted bronze, 15⅝" long. The Joseph H. Hirshhorn Collection. Ill. p. 35

7 *Standing Man.* 1930. Plaster, 26" high. The Joseph H. Hirshhorn Collection

*8 *Suspended Ball.* 1930-31. Wood and metal, 23⅝" high. Private collection. Ill. p. 36

*9 *Disagreeable Object.* 1931. Wood, 19" long. Collection Mr. and Mrs. James Johnson Sweeney. (NY). Ill. p. 37

*10 *Hand Caught by a Finger (Main prise).* 1932. Wood and metal, 23" long. Museum of Fine Arts, Zurich. Ill. p. 37

*11 *Woman with Her Throat Cut (Femme égorgée).* 1932. Bronze, 34½" long. The Museum of Modern Art, New York. Purchase. Ill. p. 38

*12 *The Palace at 4 A.M.* 1932-33. Construction in wood, glass, wire, string, 25" high x 28¼ x 15¾". The Museum of Modern Art, New York. Purchase. (NY). Ill. p. 45

*13 *No More Play.* 1933. Marble, wood, bronze, 23 x 17⅝". Collection Mr. and Mrs. Julien Levy. (NY). Ill. p. 39

*14 *Nude (Femme qui marche).* 1933-34. Bronze, 59" high. Museum of Fine Arts, Boston. Ill. p. 43

*15 *Cubist Head.* 1934-35. Bronze, 7" high. The Joseph H. Hirshhorn Collection. Ill. p. 40

*16 *Invisible Object (Hands Holding the Void).* 1934-35. Bronze, 61" high. Collection Mr. and Mrs. Lee A. Ault. Ill. p. 43

17 *Head of Isabelle.* 1936. Bronze, 11½" high. Collection Mr. and Mrs. Allan D. Emil

18 *Two Figures.* 1936. Bronze, 5½" high. Collection Mr. and Mrs. James Laughlin

*19 *Woman with the Chariot I.* 1942-43. Bronze, 61¾" high. Pierre Matisse Gallery, New York. Ill. p. 46

*20 *Figurine.* c.1945. Plaster, 1" high on plaster base, 3⅜" high x 2 x 2". Collection Mr. and Mrs. Thomas B, Hess. Ill. p. 47

*21 *Figurine.* c.1945. Plaster, 1⅜" high on plaster base, 2½" high x 1⅝ x 1⅝". Collection Mr. and Mrs. Thomas B. Hess. Ill. p. 47

22 *Femme Leonie.* 1947. Bronze, 65½" high. Private collection

*23 *Hand.* 1947. Bronze, 28¼" long. Collection Mr. and Mrs. Paul Peralta-Ramos. Ill. p. 48

*24 *Head of a Man on a Rod.* 1947. Bronze and plaster, 21¾" high. Collection Mr. and Mrs. William N. Eisendrath, Jr. (C, LA, SF). Ill. p. 50

*25 *Head of a Man on a Rod.* 1947. Bronze, 24" high. Collection Mrs. George Acheson. (NY). Ill. p. 51

*26 *Man Pointing.* 1947. Bronze, 70½" high. The Museum of Modern Art, New York. Gift of Mrs. John D. Rockefeller, 3rd. Ill. p. 49

27 *Nose.* 1947. Bronze. Head, 14½" high x 27" long; cage, 32" high x 18 x 14½". Collection Mr. and Mrs. Arthur J. Kobacher.

28 *Tall Figure I.* 1947. Bronze, 6' 7½" high. The Joseph H. Hirshhorn Collection. (NY)

*29 *Tall Figure, Half-Size.* 1947. Bronze, 52" high. The Florene May Schoenborn and Samuel A. Marx Collection. Ill. p. 42

*30 *City Square.* 1948. Bronze, 8½" high, 25⅜" long. The Museum of Modern Art, New York. Purchase. (NY). Collection Mr. and Mrs. Morton G. Neumann. (C). Ill. p. 56

31 *Tall Figure.* 1949. Bronze, 65¾" high. Collection Aimé Maeght

*32 *Three Men Walking.* 1949. Bronze, 28¼" high. Collection Mr. and Mrs. Burt Kleiner. Ill. p. 55

*33 *Walking Quickly under the Rain.* 1949. Bronze, 17⅜″ high, 32″ long. Collection Mr. and Mrs. Gordon Bunshaft. Ill. pp. 56, 57

*34 *Between Two Houses (Figurine dans une boîte entre deux boîtes qui sont des maisons).* 1950. Bronze and glass, 11¾″ high, 20″ long, 7½″ deep. Collection Mr. and Mrs. Stanley Marcus. Ill. p. 58

*35 *Chariot.* 1950. Bronze, 57″ high. The Museum of Modern Art, New York. (NY). Ill. p. 61

*36 *Composition with Seven Figures and a Head (The Forest).* 1950. Painted bronze, 22″ high. Collection Mrs. Albert H. Newman. (C). Painted bronze, The Reader's Digest Association, Pleasantville, New York. (NY). Ill. p. 54

37 *Composition with Nine Figures (The Glade).* 1950. Bronze, 23¼″ high. Collection Mr. and Mrs. Frederick Weisman. (LA)

*38 *Four Women on a Base.* 1950. Painted bronze, 31″ high. Museum of Art, Carnegie Institute, Pittsburgh. Ill. p. 60

39 *Head of Diego.* 1950. Painted bronze, 11″ high. Collection Mr. and Mrs. Jacques Gelman

*40 *The Cage.* 1950-51. Bronze, 67″ high. Collection Aimé Maeght. Ill. p. 58

*41 *Dog.* 1951. Bronze, 18″ high, base 39″ long. The Museum of Modern Art, New York. A. Conger Goodyear Fund. (NY). Collection Mr. and Mrs. Morton G. Neumann. (C). Collection Mr. and Mrs. Frederick Weisman. (LA). Ill. p. 62

*42 *Head.* 1952. Bronze, 15″ high. Collection Aimé Maeght. Ill. p. 67

*43 *Standing Nude.* 1953. Painted plaster, 8¾″ high. Private collection. Ill. p. 65

*44 *Woman.* 1953. Bronze, 19¼″ high. The Joseph H. Hirshhorn Collection. Ill. p. 65

*45 *Head of Diego.* 1954. Bronze, 13¼″ high. Collection Mr. and Mrs. Charles Zadok. Ill. p. 52

*46 *Head of Diego.* 1954. Bronze, 26½″ high. Collection Mr. and Mrs. Sidney F. Brody. (NY, C, LA). Collection Mr. and Mrs. Richard K. Weil. (SF). Ill. p. 66

*47 *Bust of Diego.* 1955. Plaster, 7½″ high. Collection Mr. and Mrs. James W. Alsdorf. (NY, C). Ill. p. 65

48 *Diego, Study from Life.* 1955. Bronze, 15⅛″ high. The Joseph H. Hirshhorn Collection.

*49 *Figure from Venice I.* 1956. Bronze, 41¼″ high. Pierre Matisse Gallery, New York. Ill. pp. 68-69

*50 *Figure from Venice II.* 1956. Painted bronze, 47½″ high. Collection Mr. and Mrs. James W. Alsdorf. Ill. pp. 68-69

*51 *Figure from Venice III.* 1956. Bronze, 46¾″ high. Collection Mr. and Mrs. Harry W. Sherwood. Ill. pp. 68-69

*52 *Figure from Venice IV.* 1956. Bronze, 45¼″ high. Pierre Matisse Gallery, New York. Ill. pp. 68-69

*53 *Figure from Venice V.* 1956. Bronze, 43¼″ high. Pierre Matisse Gallery, New York. Ill. pp. 68-69

*54 *Figure from Venice VI.* 1956. Bronze, 52″ high. Pierre Matisse Gallery, New York. Ill. pp. 68-69

*55 *Figure from Venice VII.* 1956. Bronze, 46″ high. Pierre Matisse Gallery, New York. Ill. pp. 68-69

*56 *Figure from Venice VIII.* 1956. Bronze, 47¾″ high. Pierre Matisse Gallery, New York. Ill. pp. 68-69

*57 *Figure from Venice IX.* 1956. Bronze, 44½″ high. Pierre Matisse Gallery, New York. Ill. pp. 68-69

58 *Project for a Monument.* 1956. Bronze, 18″ high. Collection Mr. and Mrs. Carter Burden

*59 *Bust of Diego.* 1957. Bronze, 24½″ high. The Joseph H. Hirshhorn Collection. Ill. p. 53

*60 *Head of Diego on Stele I.* 1958. Bronze, 63½″ high. Pierre Matisse Gallery, New York. Ill. p. 71

*61 *Head of Diego on Stele III.* 1958. Bronze, 65⅜″ high. Collection Aimé Maeght. Ill. p. 71

*62 *Leg.* 1958-59. Bronze, 7′ high. Pierre Matisse Gallery. Ill. p. 70

*63 *Woman, Shoulder Broken (Femme, épaule cassée).* 1958-59. Bronze, 27½″ high. Collection Dr. and Mrs. Leo Chalfen. Ill. p. 63

*64 *Monumental Head.* 1960. Bronze, 37½″ high. The Joseph H. Hirshhorn Collection. (NY). Ill. p. 74

*65 *Tall Figure I.* 1960. Bronze, 8′ 10¼″ high. Pierre Matisse Gallery, New York. Ill. p. 72

*66 *Tall Figure III.* 1960. Bronze, 7′ 9″ high. Collection Mr. and Mrs. Gordon Bunshaft. (NY). Ill. p. 72

*67 *Tall Figure IV.* 1960. Bronze, 8′ 10½″ high. Pierre Matisse Gallery, New York. Ill. p. 72

*68 *Walking Man I.* 1960. Bronze, 71¾″ high. Museum of Art, Carnegie Institute, Pittsburgh. Ill. p. 73

69 *Walking Man II.* 1960. Bronze, 74⅜″ high. Collection Mr. and Mrs. Percy Uris. (NY). Collection Mr. and Mrs. David Bright. (LA, SF)

*70 *Bust of Annette.* 1962. Painted bronze, 18½″ high. Private collection. Ill. p. 75

*71 *Bust of Annette IV.* 1962. Bronze, 22½″ high. Collection Sylvan and Mary Lang. Ill. p. 64

*72 *Figure Standing (13).* 1964. Bronze, 26½″ high. Pierre Matisse Gallery, New York. Ill. p. 75

PAINTINGS

*73 *Diego at Stampa.* 1921. Oil on canvas, 24¾ x 19⅝″. Collection Alberto Giacometti. Ill. p. 76

*74 *The Artist's Mother.* 1937. Oil on canvas, 23½ x 19⅝". Collection Mrs. Pierre Matisse. Ill. p. 81

75 *Portrait of Diego.* 1948. Oil on canvas, 28¾ x 23½". Collection Mr. and Mrs. Leigh B. Block

76 *Still Life (Apples).* 1948. Oil on canvas, 10 x 12". Collection Mr. and Mrs. James W. Alsdorf

*77 *Seated Man.* 1949. Oil on canvas, 30¾ x 14½". Collection Mr. and Mrs. Morton G. Neumann. Ill. p. 78

78 *Annette.* 1950. Oil on canvas, 29⅜ x 15⅛". Collection Mr. and Mrs. William S. Paley

79 *The Artist's Mother.* 1950. Oil on canvas, 35⅜ x 24". The Museum of Modern Art, New York. Acquired through the Lillie P. Bliss Bequest. Ill. p. 80

*80 *Scene from Studio Window.* 1950. Oil, 21¼ x 13¼". Collection Mr. and Mrs. James W. Alsdorf. Ill. p. 84

*81 *Seated Figure in Studio.* (1950). Oil on canvas, 39½ x 31⅞". Collection Julian J. and Joachim Jean Aberbach. Ill. p. 79

82 *Still Life.* (1950). Oil on canvas, 19 x 17". Collection Mrs. Henry Epstein

*83 *The Studio.* 1950. Oil on canvas, 25¾ x 18¼". Collection Mr. and Mrs. James W. Alsdorf. Ill. p. 83

*84 *The Artist's Mother.* (1951). Oil on canvas, 36¼ x 28¾". Collection Aimé Maeght. Ill. p. 82

*85 *Figure.* (1951). Oil on canvas, 43¼ x 20½". Collection Mr. and Mrs. Joseph Bissett. Ill. p. 86

*86 Study after the *City Square.* 1951. Oil on canvas, 24 x 19¾". Collection Mr. and Mrs. Andrew C. Ritchie. Ill. p. 87

*87 *Landscape.* 1952. Oil on canvas, 18 x 20". Collection Mr. and Mrs. Harry W. Sherwood. Ill. p. 85

88 *The Street.* 1952. Oil on canvas, 20¾ x 19¾". Private collection

89 *Portrait of Diego.* 1953-54. Oil on canvas, 18 x 13". Collection Mr. and Mrs. James W. Alsdorf

*90 *Annette.* (1954). Oil on canvas, 25½ x 21". Collection Mr. and Mrs. Arnold H. Maremont. Ill. p. 88

91 *Seated Man.* (1954). Oil on canvas, 31¾ x 25½". Private collection

*92 *Study of Heads.* 1954. Oil on canvas, 31⅞ x 23⅜". Collection Louis Clayeux. Ill. p. 86

*93 *Bottles.* 1956. Oil on canvas, 25½ x 21¼". Collection William Inge. Ill. p. 101

*94 *Sideboard (Le Buffet).* 1957. Oil on canvas, 19¾ x 24". Collection Mr. and Mrs. Joseph L. Tucker. Ill. p. 90

95 *Still Life with Fruit.* 1957. Oil on canvas, 24 x 19¾". Galerie Claude Bernard, Paris

96 *Yanaihara II.* 1956. Oil on canvas, 32 x 25½". Pierre Matisse Gallery, New York

*97 *Portrait of David Sylvester.* 1960. Oil on canvas, 45¾ x 35". Collection Mr. and Mrs. Joseph Pulitzer, Jr. Ill. p. 102

*98 *Annette.* (1961). Oil on canvas, 45¾ x 35". Collection Mr. and Mrs. Jacques Gelman. Ill. p. 89

*99 *Annette.* 1961. Oil on canvas, 21⅞ x 17¾". The Joseph H. Hirshhorn Collection. Ill. p. 103

*100 *Caroline.* 1961. Oil on canvas, 45¾ x 35". Frank and Ursula Laurens Collection. Ill. p. 91

101 *Head of Diego.* (1961). Oil on canvas, 17¾ x 13¾". Museum of Fine Arts, Boston

*102 *Head of a Man.* (1961). Oil on canvas, 19 x 16". Collection Mr. and Mrs. Sidney L. Solomon. Ill. p. 92

103 *Caroline.* 1962. Oil on canvas, 36¼ x 28¾". Collection Mr. and Mrs. Henry A. Markus

*104 *Caroline.* 1962. Oil on canvas, 39¼ x 32". Collection Mr. and Mrs. Robert B. Mayer. Ill. p. 104

*105 *Head.* (1962). Oil on canvas, 36¼ x 28¾". Collection Aimé Maeght. Ill. p. 93

106 *Portrait of James Lord.* 1964. Oil on canvas, 46 x 32". Collection James Lord

DRAWINGS

*107 *Portrait of Simon Bérard.* (c.1918). Pen and ink, 12¼ x 9¼". Collection James Lord. Ill. p. 94

*108 *Self-Portrait.* 1937. Pencil, 19¼ x 12¼". Collection Pierre Matisse. Ill. p. 94

*109 *Head of a Woman.* 1946. Crayon, 19½ x 13¾" (sight). Private collection. Ill. p. 95

*110 *Figures on City Square.* 1947. Pencil, 12⅞ x 20". Collection Gene R. Summers. Ill. p. 96

*111 *Standing Nude.* (1947). Oil on paper, 24¾ x 13½" Collection Eleanor Ward. Ill. p. 96

112 *Standing Woman.* 1947. Pencil, 21¼ x 14½". Private collection

113 *Two Male Figures and Standing Nude.* 1948. Pencil, 17¾ x 11⅜". Collection Mr. and Mrs. Eugene Victor Thaw

*114 *Jean-Paul Sartre.* 1949. Pencil, 11½ x 8⅞". Collection Ruth and Hermann Vollmer. Ill. p. 106

*115 *Walking Man.* (c.1950). Oil on paper, 26¾ x 20". Collection James Lord. Ill. p. 97

*116 *Bust on Sculpture Stand.* 1951. Crayon, 22 x 14⅜". Collection Ruth and Hermann Vollmer. Ill. p. 98

117 *Five Tall Figures.* 1951. Lithographic crayon, 15⅜ x 11". Collection Dr. and Mrs. Werner Muensterberger

*118 *Interior.* 1951. Pencil, 14½ x 10¼". Private collection. Ill. p. 99

119 *Interior with Nude.* 1951. Crayon, 15 x 21¾". Collection Ruth and Hermann Vollmer

*120 *Tree.* 1952. Pencil, 20 x 13½". Collection Mr. and Mrs. James W. Alsdorf. Ill. p. 108

121 *Landscape.* 1953. Pencil, 11½ x 16¼". B. C. Holland Gallery, Inc., Chicago

122 *Seated Man* (Peter Watson). 1953. Pencil, 19¾ x 12¾". Collection Mr. and Mrs. James W. Alsdorf

*123 *Henri Matisse–Nice.* June 30, 1954. Pencil, 18½ x 12⅜". Collection Alberto Giacometti. Ill. p. 106

124 *Henri Matisse.* July 6, 1954. Pencil, 18¾ x 12¼". Collection Alberto Giacometti

125 *Seated Woman.* (1954). Pencil, 18¼ x 12¼". Collection Mr. and Mrs. Philip Gersh

126 *Portrait of Marilynn Alsdorf.* 1955. Pencil, 19½ x 12¾". Collection Mr. and Mrs. James W. Alsdorf

*127 *Self-Portrait.* (1955). Pencil, 19¼ x 12½". Private collection. Ill. p. 107

*128 *Annette in the Studio.* 1956. Pen and ink, 14 x 9½". Collection Mr. and Mrs. James W. Alsdorf. Ill. p. 98

*129 *The Dormer Window.* 1957. Pencil, 25⅝ x 19¾". Courtesy The Museum of Modern Art, New York. Ill. p. 99

*130 *Igor Stravinsky.* 1957. Pencil, 15⅞ x 12". Collection Mr. and Mrs. Robert D. Graff. Ill. p. 107

*131 *Mountain.* 1957. Pencil, 19¾ x 25¾". The Solomon R. Guggenheim Museum, New York. Ill. p. 109

*132 Sketch page. 1959. Pencil and colored crayon, 14¼ x 10½". Collection Dr. and Mrs. Werner Muensterberger. Ill. p. 105

*133 *Vase of Flowers.* 1959. Pencil, 19⅝ x 12⅝". Private collection. Ill. p. 100

134 *Bust of a Man.* 1960. Pencil, 19¾ x 12¾". Collection Steven N. Kaufmann

135 *Head of Diego.* (1960). Ball point pen, 7⅛ x 3⅝". Collection Larry G. Hager

*136 *Head of a Man and Torso of a Woman.* (1962). Ball point pen on paper napkin, 9¾ x 4¾", irreg. Collection Ruth and Hermann Vollmer. Ill. p. 110

137 *Portrait of Alice.* (1962). Ball point pen, 6¼ x 3½". Collection Mr. and Mrs. John Rewald

*138 *Self-Portrait.* (1962). Ball point pen on paper napkin, 7¼ x 5", irreg. Collection Ruth and Hermann Vollmer. Ill. p. 111

*139 *Three Heads.* 1962. Ball point pen, 8⅛ x 6". Collection Pierre Matisse. Ill. p. 110

140 *Figure in an Interior.* 1963. Pencil, 19⅝ x 12¾". Private collection

Three busts of Diego. (c. 1957).

Julian J. and Joachim Jean Aberbach; Mrs. George Acheson; Mr. and Mrs. James W. Alsdorf; Mr. and Mrs. Lee A. Ault; Mr. and Mrs. Joseph Bissett; Mr. and Mrs. Leigh B. Block; Mr. and Mrs. David B. Bright; Mr. and Mrs. Sidney F. Brody; Mr. and Mrs. Gordon Bunshaft; Mr. and Mrs. Carter Burden; Dr. and Mrs. Leo Chalfen; Louis Clayeux; Mr. and Mrs. William N. Eisendrath, Jr.; Mr. and Mrs. Allan D. Emil; Mrs. Henry Epstein; Mr. and Mrs. Jacques Gelman; Mr. and Mrs. Philip Gersh; Alberto Giacometti; Mr. and Mrs. Robert D. Graff; Larry G. Hager; Mr. and Mrs. Thomas B. Hess; The Joseph H. Hirshhorn Collection; William Inge; Steven N. Kaufmann; Mr. and Mrs. Burt Kleiner; Sylvan and Mary Lang; Mr. and Mrs. James Laughlin; Frank and Ursula Laurens Collection; Mr. and Mrs. Julien Levy; James Lord; Aimé Maeght; Mr. and Mrs. Stanley Marcus; Mr. and Mrs. Arnold H. Maremont; Mr. and Mrs. Henry A. Markus; Mrs. Pierre Matisse; Mr. and Mrs. Pierre Matisse; Mr. and Mrs. Robert B. Mayer; Dr. and Mrs. W. Muensterberger; Mr. and Mrs. Morton G. Neumann; Mrs. Albert H. Newman; Mr. and Mrs. William S. Paley; Mr. and Mrs. Paul Peralta-Ramos; Mr. and Mrs. Joseph Pulitzer, Jr.; The Reader's Digest Association; Mr. and Mrs. John Rewald; Mr. and Mrs. Andrew C. Ritchie; The Florene May Schoenborn and Samuel A. Marx Collection; Mr. and Mrs. Harry Sherwood; Mr. and Mrs. Sidney L. Solomon; Dr. and Mrs. Frank Stanton; Gene R. Summers; Mr. and Mrs. James Johnson Sweeney; Mr. and Mrs. Eugene Victor Thaw; Mr. and Mrs. Joseph L. Tucker; Mr. and Mrs. Percy Uris; Ruth and Hermann Vollmer; Eleanor Ward; Mr. and Mrs. Richard K. Weil; Mr. and Mrs. Frederick Weisman; Mr. and Mrs. Harry Lewis Winston; Mr. and Mrs. Charles Zadok.

Museum of Fine Arts, Boston; The Art Institute of Chicago; The Solomon R. Guggenheim Museum, New York; The Museum of Modern Art, New York; Museum of Art, Carnegie Institute, Pittsburgh; Museum of Fine Arts, Zurich.

Galerie Claude Bernard, Paris; B. C. Holland Gallery, Inc., Chicago; Pierre Matisse Gallery, New York.

Drawing for the jacket by Alberto Giacometti, 1965.